HOW DOES IT WORK?

by Dru Hunter

CREATIVE EDUCATION • CREATIVE PAPERBACKS

Published by **Creative Education** and **Creative Paperbacks**
P.O. Box 227, Mankato, Minnesota 56002
Creative Education and Creative Paperbacks are imprints of The Creative Company
www.thecreativecompany.us

Design and production by **Christine Vanderbeek**
Art direction by **Rita Marshall**
Printed in the Malaysia

Photographs by Corbis (CARLO ALLEGRI/Reuters, H. Lorren Au Jr/ZUMA Press, Bettmann, Stefano Bianchetti, Victor R. Caivano/AP, Christie's Images, Joseph Siffred Duplessis/Bettmann, NIR ELIAS/Reuters, Peter Ginter/Science Faction, Mark Hanauer, Hulton-Deutsch Collection, Layne Kennedy, KEVIN LAMARQUE/Reuters, Leemage, CHARLES W LUZIER/Reuters, Philadelphia Museum of Art, Science Photo Library), Dreamstime (Anne Power), Getty Images (NASA/Handout, NASA-Apollo/digital version by Science Faction, Stock Montage), iStockphoto (7activestudio, GeorgiosArt, imgendesign, justinkendra, Orientaly, rypson, TibiP03, TonyBaggett), Shutterstock (cherezoff, Georgios Kollidas, Marina Sun, Daria Minaeva, pirtuss, Praisaeng, Eugene Sergeev, SurangaSL, vitals)

Library of Congress Cataloging-in-Publication Data
Hunter, Dru.
How does it work? / Dru Hunter.
p. cm. — (Think like a scientist)
Includes bibliographical references and index.
Summary: A narration of the origins, advancements, and future of the physical sciences, including chemistry and physics, and the ways in which scientists utilize the scientific method to explore questions.

ISBN 978-1-60818-593-1 (hardcover)
ISBN 978-1-62832-198-2 (pbk)
1. Science—Methodology—Juvenile literature. 2. Scientists—Juvenile literature. 3. Technology—History—Juvenile literature. I. Title.

Q175.2.H866 2015
500—dc23   2014030809

CCSS: RI.5.1, 2, 3, 8; RI.6.1, 3, 7; RST.6-8.1, 2, 5, 6, 8

First Edition HC 9 8 7 6 5 4 3 2 1
First Edition PBK 9 8 7 6 5 4 3 2 1

ON THE COVER **The space shuttle *Atlantis* blasting off from Kennedy Space Center in June 2007**

TABLE OF CONTENTS

SCIENTIST IN THE SPOTLIGHT

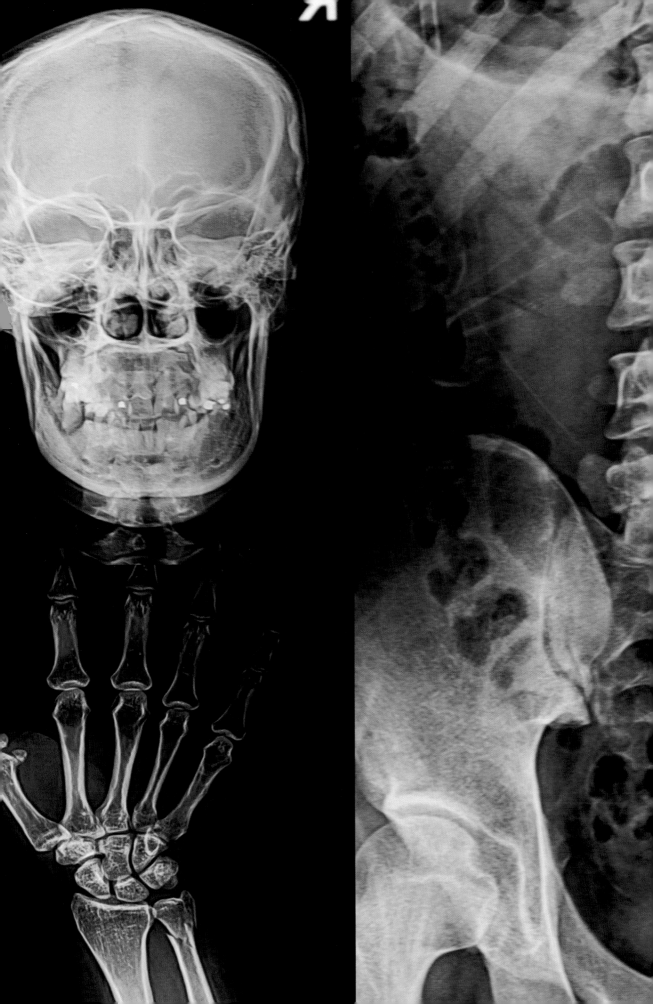

INTRODUCTION

A screen across the room was glowing. Physicist Wilhelm Röntgen wondered what was going on. He was experimenting with cathode ray tubes (similar to modern light bulbs).

Röntgen had placed an electric volt through each cathode tube. The tubes glowed, even when he covered them with paper. That was when he noticed the green light glowing on the screen and realized he had created a new type of light ray. His ray was passing through solid materials—something that should have been impossible! He wondered whether it would penetrate other subjects: What would happen if he tried to pass his new ray through the human body? Röntgen placed his wife's hand over a photographic plate and cast the ray. An image of her bones and wedding ring appeared on the plate. It was 1895, and Röntgen had just taken the first X-ray!

Physical science is all about how things work in nature. Physics studies the most basic forces at work in our world and universe. It deals with the relationships between **matter** and energy. Chemistry looks deeper into the structure of that matter, examining how substances interact with energy and one another. In using the **scientific method**, a physical scientist understands how something works by asking questions and making observations. Experiments in the physical sciences give people a closer look at the world's inner workings and can lead to important problem-solving discoveries. From X-rays of broken bones to the chemistry needed to make TVs and phones work, everything in our world runs on the physical sciences.

EUREKA MOMENTS

MANY CONSIDER PHYSICS TO BE THE OLDEST science. Physics covers a wide range of subjects from the smallest atomic particle to enormous galaxies. Physicists, scientists who study physics, conduct research in subjects such as electricity, astronomy, forces, light, and sound. Objects on our planet and throughout our universe affect each other, so it is the job of some physicists to study these interactions. Much of the technology we use today comes from discoveries physicists have made in the last few centuries.

Since ancient times, people have noticed and attempted to understand the extraordinary natural occurrences or events around them. When they looked up at what was happening in the sky, they tried to explain the concepts of night and day. When they observed the seasons, they invented reasons for those as well.

In 1400s Europe, explanations for the changing seasons and how day turned into night involved the belief that Earth was the

Observations of the universe led to theories of its physical makeup and workings.

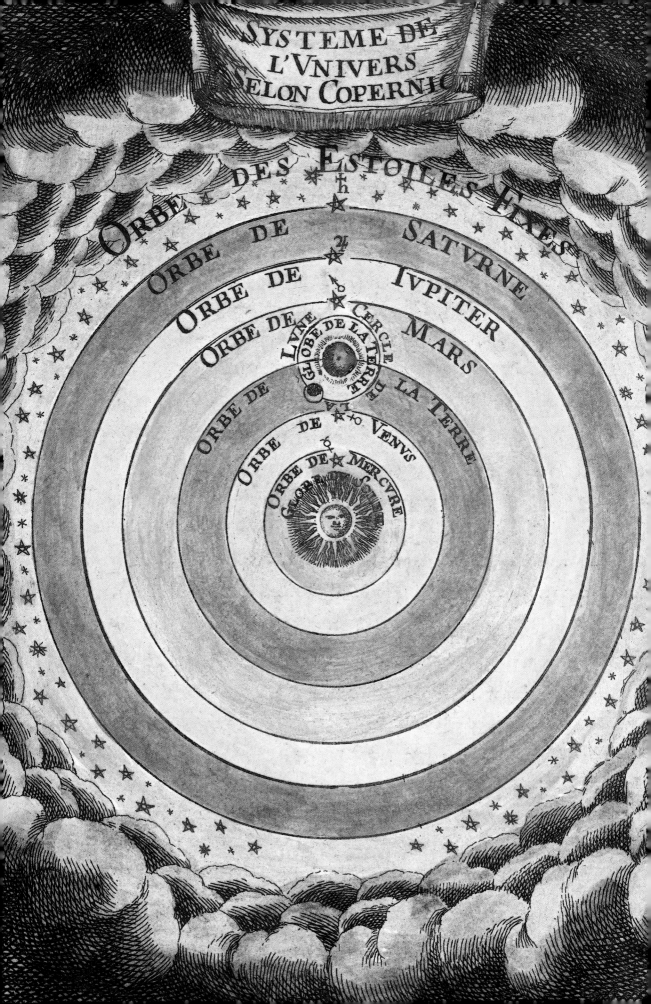

center of the entire universe and everything revolved around it. Some even believed that stars were tiny, glass-filled holes in the night sky. Nicolaus Copernicus, a Polish student of astronomy and mathematics, found flaws in what he was taught and began to ask questions. What if everything humans believed about how our universe worked was wrong? Copernicus gained as much knowledge as he could, even working as an assistant to an astronomer in 1496.

In secret, Copernicus worked on his **hypothesis**. He believed Earth and the planets **orbited** the sun. Known as "heliocentric theory," this was in direct opposition to what was taught at the time. Some historians suggest Copernicus did not want to publish his findings because of possible objections from scholars.

After nearly 30 years of study and observation, Copernicus finally allowed his heliocentric theory to be published in a book titled *On the Revolutions of the Heavenly Spheres*. In it, he described the yearlong path of Earth around the sun and explained how the motions of the planets were elliptical rather than circular (as the ancient Greeks had claimed). He also discussed how Earth rotated on its axis, causing the seasons, and the positions in the universe of the five planets he could observe. Copernicus estimated the distance from Earth to the sun was closer than the distance between Earth and what he called "fixed stars." Printed the year of his death (A.D. 1543), Copernicus's book influenced Galileo Galilei, an Italian physicist, mathematician, and astronomer who faced opposition for his own research in the 1600s.

Galileo was particularly interested in the science of motion. He hypothesized that if a heavy object and a lighter object were dropped from the same distance, they both would land at the same time despite the weight of the heavier object. According to an account by one of Galileo's students, to test his theory, Galileo

Copernicus (above) may have erred in his ideas about "fixed stars," but his sun-centered model (opposite) was correct.

BENJAMIN FRANKLIN

One of America's Founding Fathers, Benjamin Franklin (1706–90) was also a scientist. The 10th son of 17 children born to a family in Boston, Massachusetts, Franklin left Boston to work in the printing business in Philadelphia, Pennsylvania. After his publishing career took off, he became famous for his inventions, such as the Franklin stove. He did not **patent** any of his inventions because he said he invented them to improve society. Franklin's experiments with electricity produced another invention. To test whether lightning was a form of electricity, Franklin attached a metal key to a kite and flew it into a rain cloud in June 1752. He survived his risky experiment and proved lightning was made up of streaks of electrified air. Franklin then invented the lightning rod, which is still used today to help protect people, ships, and buildings by drawing electricity to the ground.

dropped 2 balls of different weights approximately 186 feet (56.7 m) from the Leaning Tower of Pisa, a cathedral bell tower in Italy. Both balls landed at the same time, proving the point.

Galileo built his own telescope in 1609 to study the universe. He observed the Milky Way and found it filled with stars that appeared to be at different distances from the earth. This debunked the belief that Earth was a glass sphere with stars equidistant from it. Galileo also observed the moon's craters, valleys, and mountains, disproving the belief that it was a perfectly smooth, round ball. Studying the planet Jupiter, Galileo discovered four moons, which he called "stars," orbiting it. This led him to claim that there was new support for the heliocentric theory.

People responded in different ways to Galileo's astronomical findings. Some were excited to discover more, while others could not believe it. Later, when Galileo tried to show that heliocentrism was consistent with biblical writings, a group of officials in the Catholic Church told Galileo he was not allowed to defend heliocentrism on such a basis. When Galileo published a book in 1632 and compared Copernicus's theory with the Ptolemaic system (a mathematical model of the universe), the governing body of the Church sentenced him to life in prison.

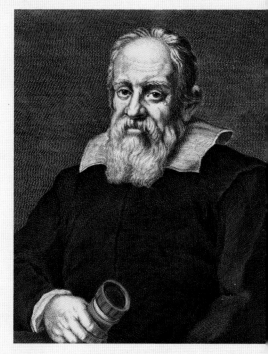

Galileo's emphasis on experimentation—testing one's ideas—revealed a new way of approaching science.

Along with ideas about the workings of the universe, the ancient Greeks had come up with early explanations for its chemical make-up. Chemistry is often called the "central science" because of its importance in linking physical sciences with life and applied sciences. Scientists who study chemistry are called chemists. Chemistry is not only performed in a lab, it is found in nature all around us. Food is grown through chemistry. When we eat at a restaurant, chefs make

DID YOU KNOW? The aurora borealis (above), or Northern Lights, is a natural display of electricity

use of chemistry to ensure a great meal. We are able to understand the air we breathe and what we can see, feel, and taste because of chemistry. We are also able to understand more about ourselves.

In ancient history, chemistry was focused on finding ways to change common metals such as lead into gold. Alchemists were also trying to make concoctions that, when ingested, would give the person eternal life. What they discovered along the way, though, was how to shape metals into better and stronger blends and to mix plants to cure certain sicknesses and prolong life.

Joseph Priestley was an English clergyman and chemist in the 1700s who had some outspoken political views. His support for the American and French Revolutions angered some in England so much that they burned down his church and home in 1791. Three years later, he moved to Pennsylvania, where he became reacquainted with statesman and scientist Benjamin Franklin. The two had met earlier in England while Priestley was writing *The History and Present State of Electricity.* Inspired by Franklin's and others' electrical experiments, Priestley moved from a serious study of electricity to experiments involving gases (the gases that surround Earth).

One of Priestley's most groundbreaking experiments involved using a magnifying glass to direct the sun's rays on a sample of mercuric oxide, a **compound** that is solid at room temperature. He discovered that, by heating the compound, it produced a gas that made a candle flame burn brighter. He tested the gas on mice, trapping them in a container filled with the gas. The gas seemed to keep them alive longer than the normal atmosphere. The gas Priestley had discovered was oxygen.

Before he encountered oxygen (and other gases, such as nitric oxide and ammonia), Priestley discovered carbonated water by applying gas to water in 1767. A few years later, in 1772, he published

Directions for Impregnating Water with Fixed Air. Despite inventing the first drinkable soda water, he did not try to make money from it. However, other scientists have made fortunes with their discoveries. Years after Priestley's work, 18-year-old English chemist William Henry Perkin became a multimillionaire when his chemistry experiment resulted in an unexpected discovery.

In 1856, the young Perkin was challenged by his professor at the Royal College of Chemistry to make an anti-malaria drug. After a series of experiments, Perkin made what looked like a blackened solid. It appeared to be a failed experiment until Perkin cleaned the flask and noticed the purple colors. This was something new. Perkin had made the first **synthetic** chemical dye, a substance he named mauveine (for its mauve, or pale purple, color).

Before Perkin's purple synthetic dye, the only way the color purple could be made naturally was from the mucus gland of some mollusks. Mauveine could dye silk and other textiles much more easily and soon was in worldwide demand. Patenting his chemical discovery, Perkin became wealthy in a short time and sold his company to build a large lab for himself. He spent the rest of his life studying organic chemistry and discovered more synthetic dyes as well as the basis for synthetic perfume. That simple desire to learn "how it works" continues to generate life-changing discoveries.

Natural purple dye was so rare that only royals could use it; carbonated water is today commonplace.

TRY IT OUT! Create a charge out of static electricity. Run a plastic comb through dry hair several times. Then hold the comb over small pieces of torn tissue paper. Watch the pieces of paper move like a magic trick!

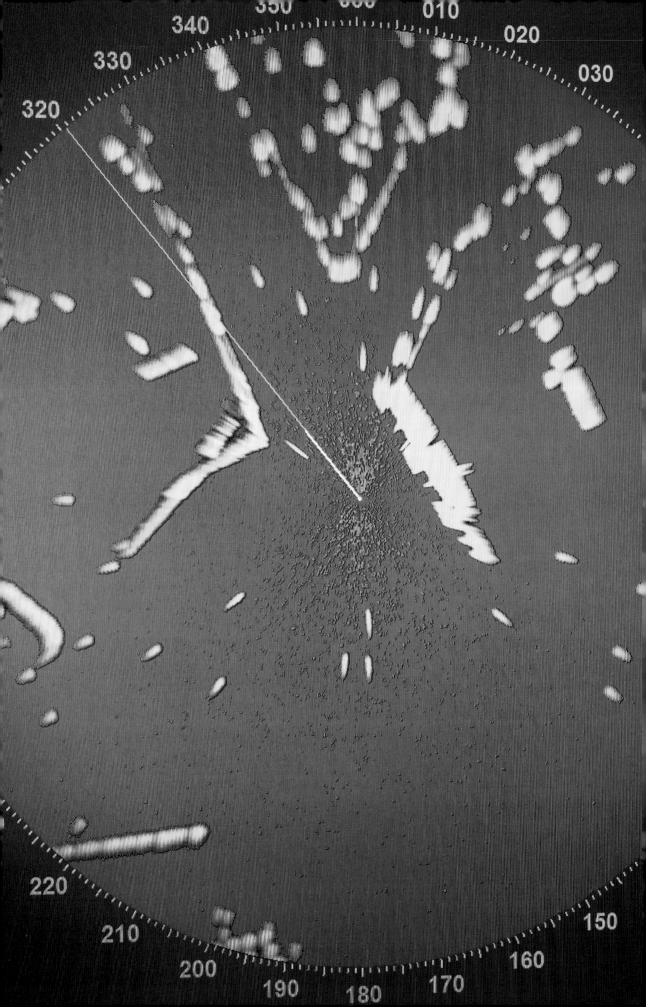

PHYSICAL SCIENCE CHANGES LIVES

SCIENTISTS LEARN FROM PAST DISCOVERIES, AND their questions about those findings often lead to further experiments or unexpected discoveries. Scottish physicist Robert Watson-Watt, a descendant of the famous steam engine inventor James Watt, began work at age 15 analyzing thunderstorms for the London Meteorological Society. Later, while working for Britain's Meteorological Office, his experiments led to the 1919 creation of an **echolocation** device.

In the 1930s, Britain became worried about Germany's growing military strength. There were rumors that Germany had a weapon that ran on radio waves. Watson-Watt and his coworkers did not think such a device was possible. However, Watson-Watt believed radio waves could be used to detect enemy airplanes. On February

Radar on a ship helps the vessel chart its course to avoid running into others.

26, 1935, he tested his hypothesis on a British bomber aircraft from six miles

(9.7 km) away. Within a few years, the radio detection and ranging system later known as radar could find an airplane that was as far as 62 miles (99.8 km) away.

Britain soon had radar towers doing around-the-clock surveillance of the country's borders. There were 20 stations up and running by the time World War II began in 1939. It is this radar that is credited with saving lives and allowing Britain to respond to German air raids. After the Japanese attack on Pearl Harbor in 1941, Watson-Watt visited the United States to consult on radar defensive strategy. Knighted in 1942 for his role in the development of radar, Watson-Watt later noted that the invention had its draw-backs: in 1956, he received a speeding ticket from a police-man who had recorded his speed using a radar gun!

Scientists since Watson-Watt have improved upon his work and the discoveries of others. Now radar is also used for mapping the earth and other planets and in tracking weather pat-terns and storms. The military uses radar to guide weapons. When the doors open automatically for you at a store, this is a form of radar, too.

The naval destroyer USS Kidd (left) was named for a victim of the Pearl Harbor attack; Watson-Watt (above) was memorialized with a statue in 2014.

Physical science discoveries have also helped save the lives of animals. An elephant's tusks, made of ivory, are actually the animal's incisor teeth grown out past its mouth. The elephant uses its tusks as weapons or tools. The teeth are embedded in the skull, with nerve endings sometimes extending all the way to the tips. Taking an ani-mal's tusks is a harmful process. In the 1800s, thousands of elephants were killed each year for their tusks. The ivory was used to make objects such as piano keys and billiard balls. American inventor John Wesley Hyatt used his knowledge of chemistry to find a substitute for ivory.

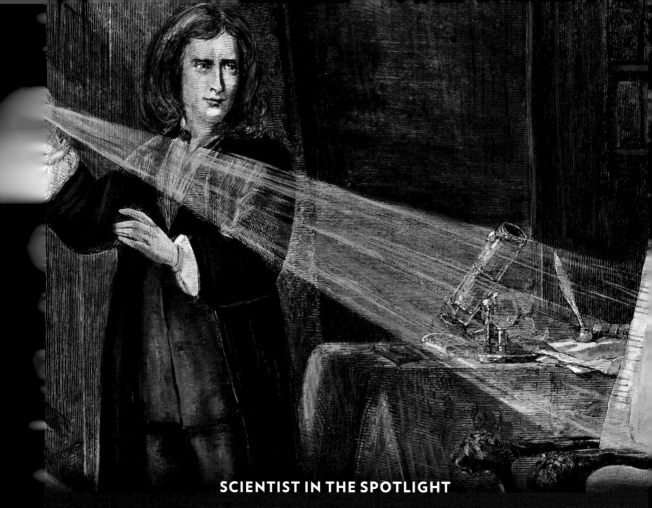

SIR ISAAC NEWTON

Often regarded as the "Father of Physics," Sir Isaac Newton was born in England in 1643. At age 17, he tried to support his family by farming but returned to school instead. He graduated from Trinity College, Cambridge, and was given a four-year scholarship for his master's degree. However, the Great Plague hit England, and Cambridge closed for 18 months. Newton used the time to come up with new theories about mathematics and physics. After watching an apple fall to the ground, Newton is said to have developed his theory of gravity. Newton made many more discoveries in optics, celestial mechanics, and mathematical fields such as calculus before taking a post at the Royal Mint for the last 30 years of his life. His 1687 *Mathematical Principles of Natural Philosophy* discusses his three laws of motion and gravity. Today, the book is considered one of the most important works of

Early chemists often used animal blood and eggs to make a substance that could bind plywood. The first man-made plastic, called Parkesine, was patented in 1856. Because Parkesine was dangerously flammable and of poor quality, it did not become widely used. Nonetheless, it did lay the groundwork for Hyatt to discover celluloid, a plastic he created by combining solid and liquid forms of Parkesine. Once the new material was patented, celluloid was used to replace ivory in billiard balls, piano keys, and combs. It is still used today in Ping-Pong balls.

Hyatt's celluloid discovery in turn influenced Belgium-born chemist Leo Baekeland. Baekeland developed a type of paper he called Velox that allowed photograph development using artificial light. Eastman Kodak bought the company Baekeland was a partner in, which included the rights to his Velox invention. As a way to make money, Baekeland then turned his chemistry knowledge to developing hard plastics that could be molded. The material called Bakelite received a patent in 1909. One of the first popular plastics, it was used to make everything from buttons to radios to furniture. It is still used today in applications such as automotive brakes and parts for spacecraft.

In the 1920s and '30s, makers of rotary dial telephones adopted Bakelite as their preferred material.

Physical science is also required for getting spacecraft, such as a space shuttle, into space. Rocket engines can generate more than 3 million pounds (13.3 million Newtons) of thrust at launch. As gas is released at one end, it pushes the rocket in the opposite direction, propelling it into space. Most scientists describe the distance of 62 miles (99.8 km) above the earth as where space begins. As early as 1903, scientists speculated that reaching space using chemical fuel would require a rocket made up of several stages. Scientists over the decades further developed this hypothesis.

To stay in orbit, an object must maintain a speed of about 18,000

DID YOU KNOW? The speed that sound travels—1,127 feet (343.4 m) per second—was exceeded by the aircraft Bell X-1 in 1947.

An F-18 approaching the speed of sound, creating a vapor cone (left); the 1969 moon landing (above).

miles (28,968 km) per hour. In 1957, the Soviets' *Sputnik 1* became the first satellite to orbit Earth. The metal structure measured 23 inches (58.4 cm) and had 4 radio antennae sending pulses that could be detected around the world. After three months of circling Earth, the satellite burned up as it reentered the atmosphere.

Then came Russian cosmonaut Yuri Gagarin, who made the first human spaceflight in the Soviets' *Vostok 1* in April 1961. He went around Earth once. One month later, U.S. president John F. Kennedy made a public commitment to land a man on the moon before the end of the decade. The recently formed National Aeronautics and Space Administration (NASA) set out to train astronauts and produce vehicles that could take people beyond Earth orbit.

Apollo was an ambitious moon-landing program. It required some of the best physical scientists in the U.S. to discover how humans could get all the way to the moon and safely back to Earth. In 1967, in the very first test of the lunar module (the unit that would land on the moon), three astronauts were killed in a fire. After many changes were made to improve safety, Apollo 11 rocketed into space July 16, 1969, on the most powerful rocket yet, the Saturn V.

The three astronauts on board were commander Neil Armstrong, lunar module pilot Edwin "Buzz" Aldrin, and command module pilot Michael Collins. They spent 3 days traveling 24,200 miles (38,946 km) per hour, reaching the moon on July 19.

The following day, Aldrin and Armstrong got into their lunar module, *Eagle*, and left Collins to orbit the spaceship *Columbia* until they returned. Armstrong had to manually pilot *Eagle* to avoid a crater, and they landed about 3.7 miles (6 km) from their original intended target. "Houston, the *Eagle* has landed," Armstrong said.

At 10:39 P.M. (Eastern Standard Time), Armstrong climbed down

Eagle's 10-foot (3 m), 9-step ladder. He moved slowly and cautiously because of all the life support and communications equipment on his space suit. As he set his left foot down on the moon's surface, Armstrong's words were televised for all the world to witness: "That's one small step for [a] man; one giant leap for mankind."

Armstrong took samples of the moon's rocks and soil. After Aldrin joined him, they hoisted an American flag. They performed scientific experiments, such as setting up a foil-looking device to collect samples from the solar wind and seismic detectors to record if there were moonquakes or meteorite impacts. After about 24 hours on the moon's surface, they redocked with *Columbia*, still manned by astronaut Collins.

The return trip to Earth lasted about 60 hours, and the astronauts landed in the Pacific Ocean near Hawaii. Five more missions traveled to the moon until the Apollo program ended in 1972. The moon rocks brought back are estimated at 3.7 billion years old. Left behind on the moon was an American flag, a TV camera, two photography cameras, experiment devices, and a plaque on the lunar module's leg with a map of Earth. It bears the inscription: *Here men from the planet Earth first set foot upon the moon, July 1969* A.D. *We came in peace for all mankind.* Physical science had once again changed life on Earth—and beyond.

Supporting Apollo 11's three-stage, 363-foot (111 m) Saturn V rocket was a sturdy steel launch tower.

TRY IT OUT! Test acidity levels of water around your house with pool kit pH test strips. Record the levels and compare the pH of water from a tap in your kitchen, a pool (if you have one), a birdbath or puddle, a fish tank, and a bottle.

OLYMPIC GOLD PHYSICAL SCIENCE

N 2012, NEW YORK METS PITCHER R. A. DICKEY THREW back-to-back one-hitters, something that had not been done in 23 years. He did it by perfecting the physics of the most elusive and difficult baseball pitch that a batter can face: the knuckleball. A masterful knuckleball can rise up and down as much as a foot (30.5 cm) before it crosses home plate. The stitches around the baseball, combined with the pitcher's finger placement when the ball is released, create air turbulence. Because it lacks spin and seemingly moves at random as it makes its way to the batter, the knuckleball is one of the hardest pitches to control. However, Dickey has it down to a science.

Dr. Alan Nathan, a professor of physics at the University of Illinois, has studied Dickey's knuckleball and that of other great professional baseball pitchers. He determined that what

Pitcher R. A. Dickey was with the Mets from 2010 through the 2012 season.

Dickey does differently from the others has to do with the power behind his knuckleball. The average speed of Dickey's knuckleballs was around 77 miles (124 km) per hour—about 10 miles (16.1 km) per hour faster than Boston Red Sox great Tim Wakefield. Achieving such speed was no accident. Dickey spent years experimenting with his technique and honing the physics behind speeding up his pitch.

Dr. Nathan says, "Contrary to popular belief, knuckleball **trajectories** are as smooth as those from normal pitches. However, the data also show that the deflection of a knuckleball from a straight-line trajectory is essentially random in both magnitude and direction." The scientists found that by throwing the ball harder, Dickey gained more accuracy in his pitches, leading to more strikes.

From soccer (opposite) to baseball (above), understanding how and why balls move can improve athletes' performance in the sports.

There are lots of sports to study, let alone play and watch, from racing events to Monday Night Football to the Olympics. Professional and amateur sporting is a multibillion-dollar worldwide industry. In the U.S. alone, sports are an important part of the economy, with an estimated 1 percent of the population employed as athletes, coaches, and even sports scientists. These types of scientists can help athletes improve their performance by educating them on the physics of motion. Dr. John Eric Goff, a physics professor at Virginia's Lynchburg College and author of *Gold Medal Physics*, spent a year in England carrying out experiments in soccer physics to do just that.

One of the experiments Goff undertook with the University of Sheffield's Dr. Matt Carré involved launching soccer balls from a machine while two cameras recorded the balls' flight paths. The scientists wanted to discover more about the spin on soccer balls, including why balls with top spin in flight dip. While other scientists had carried out similar experiments in wind tunnels, Goff and Carré

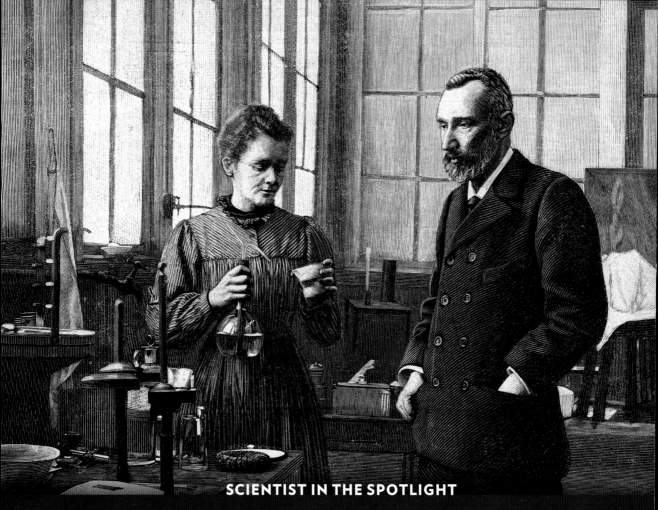

MARIE CURIE

Marie Curie (1867–1934) was born in Warsaw, Poland. When she was 24, she went to France to study at the University of Paris. There she earned degrees in physics and mathematics and met fellow scientist Pierre Curie. The two married and supported each other's work, eventually joining forces and using tools of Pierre's invention to test for **radioactivity** in all the known chemical ores. In 1903, Marie became the first woman in Europe to earn a doctorate in physics. That same year, Marie and her husband won the Nobel Prize in Physics for their work on radioactivity. At first, the prize committee did not include Marie as an award recipient, but Pierre insisted the research had been hers from the start. Awarded the 1911 Nobel Prize in Chemistry for discovering the elements radium and polonium, Marie died in 1934 from her years spent overexposed to radiation.

performed their tests in the more realistic setting of a soccer field.

They experimented with soccer balls from different orientations, launching them from varying speeds, and recorded the kinds of spins the soccer balls made. The professors also studied the aerodynamics of two different styles of soccer balls. They found that as spin increased, it began to have less effect on the ball. The results were published in the 2010 *European Journal of Physics*, and the scientists concluded that the different kinds of airflow on either side of the ball contributed to the spin factor.

The Goff/Carré experiments added to the science of how a soccer ball behaves in flight. The data they collected was made into a computer model that can teach soccer players and coaches more effective ways to score goals, such as from a penalty kick. The computer model helps them strategize the best kick to use to get around a defender and past the keeper. "This work has helped to plug a gap in some of the sets of aerodynamic data currently available for footballs [soccer balls]," said Carré. "It also helps us to understand the limits of what can be achieved by kicking balls with increasing amounts of spin. We hope that this will be of use to researchers in this field, as well as football manufacturers and coaches."

Professional athletes we watch at sporting events or on television make it look easy. When you see professional golfer Tiger Woods or Stacy Lewis sink a shot, it appears as simple as swinging a golf club and hitting the ball. However, there is a lot of physics involved in achieving the perfect golf swing.

Scientists who study the physics of a golf swing, such as New Zealand physicist Rod White, often set up cameras to capture the shot on video for later analyzing. Since the 1980s, when the first consumer camcorders came out, video has helped scientists study the physics behind sports such as golf to educate coaches and athletes.

Kicking a soccer ball off to the side puts spin on it, and it turns around its center as it moves through the air.

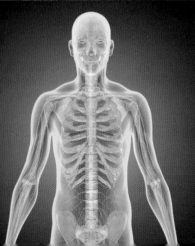

DID YOU KNOW? About two-thirds of the human body is made up of oxygen. While oxygen gas is colorless, liquid oxygen is blue.

The stages of a swing are shown by pro golfer Charles Howell III (above); an image of the skeletal and nervous systems (left).

Physicists also use radar to track the ball's speed and flight. Using these methods, they have broken down the physics of the golf swing into two main components: A golfer must first generate good swing speed from his arms and shoulders to hit the ball hard so that it goes far. Second, the golfer must let his wrists rotate freely at the correct moment while still holding the club in order to hit the ball squarely.

This wrist action in golf is an example of rotational force, or torque. If an object is not restricted while moving around in a circle, it will travel outward. This concept is similar to what happens if you are not wearing your seatbelt and the car makes a sharp left turn—you will slide to the right. When a golfer uncocks her wrists, the golf club gains additional speed, the golfer is able to apply more force (hit the ball harder), and the ball will travel farther than if she had kept her wrists rigid.

However, the real power behind a golf swing is not in the arms and wrists. The muscles in the body are what give the golfer all that energy behind the swing. When the golfer uncocks his wrists at the right stage of his swing, his body's **potential energy** is transferred to the club head in the form of **kinetic energy** moments before he strikes the ball.

Athletes around the world train hard every day to achieve one special medal: Olympic Gold. They use physics as they learn the best possible techniques. They also rely on the research of chemists for what they should eat and drink to ensure the best performance.

Athletes aren't the only ones who benefit from chemistry research. Some chemists work on trying to increase the world's food supply. They create genetically modified (GM) plant seeds to make them resistant to insects and disease. An estimated 90 percent of the corn grown on U.S. soil is GM. A lot of scientists say GM food is just as safe to eat as conventional plants, but there is controversy.

Some want more information available to the public, such as GM labels on food so that consumers know what they are eating. They also want more research on the effects GM foods have on human health and implications to the environment. With continued questions and experiments, physical scientists are seeking to improve the quality of our lives today and for future generations.

Biotechnology scientists use living things to make useful products, such as GM crops in a greenhouse.

TRY IT OUT! Make a volcano using flour, water, and newspaper strips. Let it dry overnight. Paint it. To make it chemically erupt, pour drops of red food coloring, 4 tablespoons (60 g) of baking soda, and 1 cup (237 ml) of vinegar inside the volcano. Watch the lava flow!

PHYSICAL SCIENCE OF TOMORROW

TODAY'S CHEMISTS FACE PRESSING PROBLEMS THAT affect the global population. As of 2014, an estimated 7.2 billion people lived on Earth, and that figure was expected to rise to between 8.3 and 10.9 billion by 2050. The United Nations' Food and Agriculture Organization estimates that we will need 70 percent more food than we have now to feed that expected 2050 population. Additionally, over the next 20 years, we will need about 40 percent more energy to fuel more homes and vehicles. How can scientists help address such needs?

According to the UN, 800 million people today have problems accessing clean drinking water. And about a third of the planet's peoples live in what are considered water-stressed areas. These regions have plenty of seawater but not enough means to desalt it. "The availability of water for

Approximately 50 percent of American wheat is exported to other countries.

drinking and crop irrigation is one of the most basic requirements for maintaining and improving human health," says chemist Dr. Richard Crooks from the University of Texas at Austin. Crooks partnered with Okeanos Technologies and the University of Marburg in Germany on a new way to desalinate, or desalt, seawater. Current desalting technology is expensive and easy to contaminate. "People are dying because of a lack of fresh water," says Tony Frudakis, founder and chief executive officer of Okeanos Technologies. "And they'll continue to do so until there is some kind of breakthrough, and that is what we are hoping our technology will represent." The device the chemists have developed generates a small electrical field capable of separating the salts from seawater. To run, it requires very little energy—a store-bought battery is sufficient.

Crooks and his team so far have been able to remove 25 percent of salt from a seawater sample. For water to be drinkable by humans, it needs to be 99 percent salt-free. The team is confident they will soon reach this goal with their system. But the other obstacle the chemists have to overcome is how to scale up the production so that liters of desalinated water are produced each day.

While the Texan and German chemists work on solutions to our freshwater needs, other chemists are developing drought-resistant crops, hardier seeds, and fertilizers that require less water. With more than 3 billion city-dwellers expected to crowd urban areas in 40 years, chemists are trying to develop better insulation, renewable power, and increased fuel efficiency. Lightweight cars, more effective batteries, and algae-based biofuels begin with chemistry as well. Our future cities will have to use technology to recycle all their resources and get their **carbon footprints** and

Desalination plants are built near sources such as the Mediterranean (left) and their water tested for drinkability (above).

ALBERT EINSTEIN

Albert Einstein was born in Germany in 1879. As a child, he received a compass as a gift that made him marvel at the invisible forces that moved it. In 1905, Einstein finished his doctoral degree and had five papers published in a physics journal. His fifth paper on the special theory of relativity contained his famous equation $E = mc^2$, which described how mass (the quantity of matter that forms a body, or object) could be made into large amounts of energy. After one of his other theories was proven in 1919, Einstein's fame grew, and he won a Nobel Prize in Physics in 1921. When the Nazis came to power in the 1930s, Einstein learned his name was on a list of assassination targets because of his Jewish heritage. He took a position at Princeton University in New Jersey and became an American citizen in 1940. He died in 1955, and his brain was donated to Princeton University Medical Center.

pollution down to zero. Thanks to the work of physical scientists, we have a better chance of meeting those challenges.

The International Telecommunications Union has said there are 2.7 billion people in the world today connected to the Internet. Physical scientists are making sure we have access to telecommunications, media, and music wherever we are, whether it is on the moon or in the deepest part of the ocean. With the 2014 release of Google Glass, an optical head-mounted display (OHMD), the user can search the Internet using just his or her voice. Because of the OHMD technology, some scientists think that, by 2050, we will have voiceless communication. Meanwhile, the U.S. Army is spending $6.3 million on the basic science needed to develop a "thought helmet." The new physical science behind synthetic telepathy could make it possible for soldiers, and perhaps billions of other people, to communicate with each other silently.

Google's cofounder Sergey Brin modeled an early version of the Google Glass frame in September 2012.

Looking ahead to increased populations, it is likely that chronic (long-lasting) diseases will also rise. By 2020, the U.S. could spend as much as $685 billion each year for medical costs associated with chronic diseases such as diabetes, cancer, and heart disease. Physical scientists are working on prevention, treatments, and cures.

As a California high school chemistry student, 17-year-old Angela Zhang started researching doctorate-level bioengineering papers. "At first, it was a little bit overwhelming," said Zhang, "but I found that it almost became like a puzzle, being able to decode something." Using the scientific method, she began to ask questions about possible cures for cancer. Next, she received permission to use the labs at Stanford University for her research to test her hypothesis.

Bacteria, viruses, and cells all function on a nanoscopic scale.

DID YOU KNOW? The Amazon rainforest, which covers more than 2 million square miles (5.2 million sq km) in South America, produces about 20 percent of the oxygen in Earth's atmosphere.

A nanometer is one-billionth of a meter, and to see on this level requires an instrument called an electron microscope. Zhang's idea was to mix cancer medicine in a **polymer** with nanoparticles so that the medicine would adhere to the nanoparticles. When a patient received the polymer mixture and then underwent Magnetic Resonance Imaging (MRI), the nanoparticles that attached to cancer cells would be detectable. This would allow doctors to see the precise location of cancerous tumors.

Zhang hypothesized that once doctors could identify which cells were healthy and which had cancer, an infrared light or laser could be used to melt the polymer. This would release the medicine and destroy the cancerous cells—leaving the normal healthy cells alone.

Zhang's method has been tested successfully on mice. It will take a few years still to see if it cures cancer in humans. After Zhang entered her cancer cure in the 2011 Siemens Competition in Math, Science, and Technology, she won $100,000 in college scholarships. "I'm excited to learn just everything possible," she said. "Everything in the sciences—biology, chemistry, physics, engineering, even computer science—to make new innovations possible."

Physical scientists searching for innovation also continue to examine the very existence of time and space. String theory refers to the idea that everything in the universe could be likened to musical notes on a vibrating string. Dr. Michio Kaku is a theoretical physicist and one of the founders of string field theory, a branch of string theory that searches for an explanation of the fundamental structure of the universe. According to Kaku, "the universe is a symphony of vibrating strings." Kaku has furthered legendary physicist Albert Einstein's research to bring together the four main forces of the universe known as strong and weak forces, electromagnetism, and gravity into a composite "Theory of Everything."

Kaku is also known as a futurist. Futurists try to predict what the future holds by studying trends and ideas of the present. For instance, in the future, chemistry may find a virus that can reprogram our **genes**, figure out how to slow the aging process, and make nanobots that will destroy disease and cancer cells. Chemists could also advance their techniques of making stem cells into organs that can replace old or diseased ones.

Physical scientists around the globe are working on solutions to our problems today—as well as to the projected problems of tomorrow. They start by asking the question, "Why?" They hypothesize about the possibilities. They test their hypothesis through experiments and analyze the results. Their theory may be correct, or they may need to try something new. Today, or maybe tomorrow, a physical scientist could be on the verge of making the next big discovery.

From crystals (opposite) to DNA (above), physical science studies the material structure of the world's workings.

TRY IT OUT! Grow your own **crystal**. Stir five tablespoons (75 g) of the spice alum into a cup (237 ml) of hot water. An alum crystal will become noticeable in about 30 minutes and continue growing for several hours. Try making crystals of different sizes!

carbon footprints: amounts of carbon dioxide emitted by the fossil fuel usage of an individual or group

compound: a mixture made from two or several separate items

crystal: a see-through solid that looks like ice

echolocation: a method of locating an object by sending out an echo and timing its return and the direction from which it comes

genes: hereditary units that transfer traits from a parent to a child

hypothesis: an educated guess; an explanation based on a limited amount of evidence

kinetic energy: the energy an object has from being in motion

matter: any object that takes up space and has weight

orbited: traveled a curved path revolving around objects in space

patent: to obtain a government-issued license that protects an invention from being copied by others

polymer: a large, bonded-together, chainlike molecule made up of smaller natural or synthetic molecules

potential energy: the energy an object has because of its position and potential for conversion into other kinds of energy

radioactivity: particles emitting radiation waves resulting from nuclear reactions

scientific method: a step-by-step method of research that includes making observations, forming hypotheses, performing experiments, and analyzing results

synthetic: made of artificial material resulting from a chemical reaction

trajectories: the paths flying objects follow

Calaprice, Alice, and Trevor Lipscombe. *Albert Einstein: A Biography*. Westport, Conn.: Greenwood, 2005.

Carey, Charles W. Jr. *American Inventors, Entrepreneurs, and Business Visionaries*. New York: Simon & Schuster, 2004.

Gribbin, John. *The Scientists: A History of Science Told through the Lives of Its Greatest Inventors*. New York: Random House, 2003.

Isaacson, Walter. *Benjamin Franklin: An American Life*. New York: Simon & Schuster, 2004.

Johnson, George. *The Ten Most Beautiful Experiments*. New York: Vintage Books, 2009.

Johnson, Steven. *The Invention of Air: A Story of Science, Faith, Revolution, and the Birth of America*. New York: Riverhead Books, 2009.

Kaku, Michio. *Physics of the Future*. New York: Anchor Books, 2012.

Nelson, Craig. *Rocket Men: The Epic Story of the First Men on the Moon*. New York: Viking, 2009.

LIBERTY'S KIDS
http://www.libertyskids.com/arch_who_bfranklin.html.
Learn about Benjamin Franklin and other famous men and women in history.

NASA KID'S CLUB
http://www.nasa.gov/audience/forkids/kidsclub/flash/index.html.
This website contains information about the past, present, and future U.S. space missions.

Note: Every effort has been made to ensure that the websites listed above are suitable for children, that they have educational value, and that they contain no inappropriate material. However, because of the nature of the Internet, it is impossible to guarantee that these sites will remain active indefinitely or that their contents will not be altered.